Original title:
When Love Heals

Copyright © 2024 Swan Charm
All rights reserved.

Author: Kätriin Kaldaru
ISBN HARDBACK: 978-9916-89-796-6
ISBN PAPERBACK: 978-9916-89-797-3
ISBN EBOOK: 978-9916-89-798-0

The Embrace of Grace

In shadows deep, Your love will find,
A weary soul, in heart unlined.
With open arms, You draw me near,
A gentle whisper, free from fear.

In every trial, Your strength I see,
A guiding light, You walk with me.
Through stormy nights, Your peace will flow,
Like rivers deep, in tranquil glow.

Restore My Spirit

O Lord, my heart cries out for peace,
In weary days, may strife all cease.
With every breath, I seek Your grace,
Restore my soul, in love embrace.

The burdens I hold weigh heavy still,
In Your presence, I find my will.
Renew my spirit, lift me high,
In faith and hope, I soar the sky.

The Light That Binds

In every heart, a light does gleam,
A sacred bond, a timeless dream.
With hands outstretched, we join as one,
United hearts, beneath the sun.

In kindness sown, we nurture love,
A gift from Him, who reigns above.
Through trials faced, we'll stand in grace,
In faith together, we find our place.

Sanctuary of Heartfelt Words

Within these walls, where whispers dwell,
The stories told, of heaven's spell.
With open hearts, we gather near,
In love's embrace, we cast our fear.

Each word a prayer, each voice a song,
In harmony, where we belong.
In this safe space, our spirits soar,
A sanctuary, forevermore.

Divine Light

In the stillness of the night,
Whispers of angels take flight.
Heaven's grace, a guiding star,
Leads us to where blessings are.

In the heart where faith resides,
Love and hope are gentle guides.
With each prayer, souls intertwine,
In the sacred, all is divine.

Through valleys low and mountains high,
We seek the truth, we touch the sky.
In every echo, in every sigh,
God's embrace will never lie.

With every dawn, a chance to rise,
To walk in light, beyond the skies.
In community, we find our strength,
Bound by love's eternal length.

In quiet moments, hearts align,
In still waters, spirits shine.
Together, we find His grace,
In every tear, a holy place.

From Ashes to Affection

From ashes rise, the spirit sings,
In trials deep, new hope begins.
With hearts awakened, love commands,
In grace and faith, we take our stands.

A journey vast, through shadows tread,
In every tear, the light is fed.
Through sacred bonds, we learn to heal,
In every touch, love's truth revealed.

In whispered prayers, our souls connect,
From every loss, new paths we select.
A circle formed, in trust we lay,
From ashes born, affection stays.

Blessings in the Silence

In silence deep, the spirit speaks,
A sacred space where solace seeks.
Through hushed whispers, we find our way,
In quietude, we learn to pray.

With steady hearts, we listen close,
In moments still, the grace we chose.
Each breath a gift, a blessing flows,
In silent strength, the soul just grows.

Beneath the weight of worldly noise,
In tranquil calm, we find our joys.
A gentle touch, each heart entwines,
In love's embrace, the spirit shines.

Covenant of Healing Touch

In healing touch, our spirits bind,
With every grasp, the heart aligned.
A promise kept, amid the pain,
In warmth and grace, new life we gain.

With tender hands, we break the chains,
In shared affection, love remains.
A covenant forged in humble light,
To guide us through each shadowed night.

Through gentle whispers, faith ignites,
In sacred bonds, we find our sights.
Together held, we rise anew,
As healing flows, the spirit's true.

Graced by Togetherness

In every heart, a rhythm beats,
United souls in faith, we meet.
With hands reached out, we dare to share,
In graced togetherness, love's care.

With every laugh and tear we find,
In unity, our spirit's kind.
Through trials faced, we stand as one,
In love created, the battle's won.

A tapestry of dreams we weave,
In strength of many, we believe.
Through dark and light, our journey blends,
In graced togetherness, the spirit mends.

Transcendental Touch

In silence, spirits rise and soar,
Beyond the stars, forevermore.
A gentle breeze, divine embrace,
Awakens hearts in sacred space.

In every prayer, a whisper heard,
A promise kept, a steadfast word.
With faith as light, we walk the path,
In love's vast arms, we feel the wrath.

Transcendence found in humble heart,
In unity, we play our part.
The soul ignites, a fiery glow,
In depths of grace, we come to know.

From shadows cast, we find the way,
With every dawn, a brand new day.
The touch of grace, forever near,
In every tear, the light shines clear.

Hymn of Restored Spirits

O weary souls, arise anew,
In faith's embrace, find strength so true.
Through trials faced, our hearts unite,
In harmony, we seek the light.

A hymn of peace, sweet voices blend,
In every note, our lives descend.
With every tear, a joyful sound,
Restored and healed, we stand our ground.

Through darkest nights, the stars will guide,
In whispered prayers, we won't divide.
With open hearts, we share the grace,
In every challenge, love we trace.

Through valleys deep, we journey wide,
With every step, our faith our guide.
A spirit strong, forever free,
In unity, we find our plea.

Seraphic Whispers

In fragrant blooms, the angels sing,
In heavenly notes, their praises ring.
With wings of light, they dance and play,
In whispered truths that lead the way.

The sacred hush of twilight speaks,
In tranquil peace, our spirit seeks.
Through every shadow, solace flows,
In quiet grace, our knowing grows.

With every sigh, a prayer ascends,
The heart, a vessel that no one bends.
In seraphic tunes, our souls rejoice,
In love's embrace, we find our voice.

As dawn awaits, the promise shines,
In every heart, a tale entwines.
The dance of light, a celestial fire,
Awakens hope, ignites desire.

The Healing Hands of Faith

In quiet moments, grace unfolds,
With healing hands, the heart consoled.
Through trials faced, our spirit grows,
In every touch, love's essence flows.

A gentle hand, a soft caress,
In faith's embrace, we find our rest.
Restored through prayer, our spirits mend,
In every heart, a faithful friend.

With every wound, a lesson learned,
In light of hope, our souls are turned.
Through storms that rage, the calm we seek,
In open hearts, we hear the meek.

The path of love, forever bright,
In tender moments, we find our light.
With faith as guide, we'll never fall,
In healing hands, we stand so tall.

Divine Embrace

In the silence, hearts align,
Whispers echo, love divine.
Hands extended, grace unfolds,
Warmth that comforts, truth that holds.

Beneath the stars, we find our place,
In sacred moments, we embrace.
Bound by faith, a common thread,
In every tear, a promise said.

Sacred Renewal

Morning breaks with golden light,
Hearts awaken, souls take flight.
Nature sings of life anew,
In every dawn, a promise true.

The river flows, it reflects grace,
In every ripple, love we trace.
Hands uplifted, spirits soar,
In sacred cycles, we restore.

Grace Within Shadows

In darkest nights, a flicker glows,
Silent prayers, the spirit knows.
With every doubt, a deeper trust,
In gentle hands, we find the just.

Shadows dance, but light will meet,
With every heartbeat, love's heartbeat.
Embrace the trials, rise above,
For grace abounds in endless love.

The Alchemy of Affection

From stardust dreams, connections bloom,
In simple acts, dispel the gloom.
Words like honey, soft and sweet,
In every moment, hearts compete.

Fingers weave a tapestry,
In love's embrace, we're truly free.
Through laughter shared and tears we shed,
The alchemy of love is fed.

Communion of Kindred Hearts

In the stillness of the night, we gather,
Hands entwined, spirits aflame,
Whispers of love fill the air,
In this sacred space, we proclaim.

Bound by grace, together we stand,
Hearts entwined in divine embrace,
Each beat a hymn, a soft command,
To uphold the light, to spread His grace.

In sunlit gardens, beneath His gaze,
We share our joys, our burdens laid,
Each prayer a petal in endless praise,
In unity, peace shall never fade.

Through trials faced, our faith will grow,
In every tear, a seed is sown,
Together we rise, together we glow,
For in this love, we are never alone.

A communion sacred, a bond not worn,
In every heart, a spark divine,
Kindred souls forever reborn,
In His embrace, our spirits align.

The Sacred Gift of Forgiveness

In the quiet of dawn, a lesson unfolds,
Forgiveness flows like a river wide,
Removing weights that bind our souls,
A healing balm where peace abides.

With open hearts, we share the weight,
Casting aside the chains of past,
Forging new paths through love's true gate,
In this gentle grace, we are steadfast.

Let words of mercy be our guide,
In every whisper, a promise sealed,
Together we'll walk, side by side,
In the sacred gift, our wounds are healed.

For in each act of pure release,
We find the strength to rise above,
Transforming pain into sweet peace,
In forgiveness, we discover love.

The light of faith shines ever bright,
Leading us home through darkest nights,
With open hands and hearts in flight,
We embrace the gift, our souls ignited.

Echoes of Eternal Care

In the whispers of the trees, we hear,
Echoes of love that never cease,
Kindness woven through every tear,
In our hearts, we find this peace.

Softly spoken in gentle breeze,
Care like shadows follows near,
In every breath, we seek to please,
A nurturing hand, we draw so dear.

Through storms of life, we hold each other,
In the silence, we are one,
As sisters, brothers, like no other,
In shared burdens, our journey's begun.

The sacred bond of open hearts,
In every laugh, a sacred prayer,
From small beginnings, love imparts,
The echoes of eternal care.

So let us cherish this divine thread,
That weaves us whole, banishing fear,
In each connection, where love is spread,
We find the strength to persevere.

Radiant Bonds

In the tapestry of life, love intertwines,
Radiant bonds that span the age,
Every soul a thread that shines,
Together we write our sacred page.

From every corner of this earth,
Voices rise in harmonious song,
Celebrating every heart's worth,
In diversity, we all belong.

United we stand, in hope and faith,
Casting out darkness with our light,
In every challenge, we find our strength,
Illuminating paths through the night.

Oh, let our love be a guiding star,
Leading the lost to a home so true,
In every distance, no soul too far,
In radiant bonds, we are renewed.

Forever entwined, we journey on,
In the warmth of each tender embrace,
Through trials faced, our worries gone,
In love's embrace, we find our place.

The Blossoming Heart

In stillness, the spirit grows,
A seed of love in silence sows.
From deep within the soul's embrace,
Awakens gently, finding grace.

Through trials faced, the heart finds peace,
In every moment, love's increase.
With open hands and open eyes,
The blossoming heart begins to rise.

Let kindness flow like rivers wide,
With faith and hope forever guide.
In shared connection, unity,
The blossoming heart sets spirit free.

Celestial Pathways of Healing

Beneath the stars, we seek the light,
Celestial whispers guide our plight.
In prayers spoken, love surrounds,
Healing journeys know no bounds.

With every breath, the heart will mend,
In sacred time, we find our friend.
The universe a hand extended,
In grace and truth, our pain is tended.

Each step a dance on paths divine,
Together, in spirit, we align.
Through darkened nights, the dawn will break,
Celestial pathways, hope awake.

Anointed Moments

In fleeting time, we find our grace,
Anointed moments in this space.
Each heartbeat echoes heaven's song,
A tapestry where we belong.

In sacred breath, we learn to see,
The gift of life, a mystery.
With humble hearts, we seek the light,
Anointed moments shine so bright.

Through laughter shared and tears that flow,
In every joy, the love will grow.
These cherished times, our spirits raise,
Anointed moments, endless praise.

The Embrace of Eternity

In timeless arms, the soul finds rest,
The embrace of eternity, truly blessed.
With every breath, we touch the divine,
Connected as one, spirits entwined.

Through every laughter, every tear,
In moments sacred, we draw near.
Beyond the veil where shadows play,
The embrace of love will lead the way.

In whispers soft, the truth is found,
In silence deep, our hearts unbound.
Through endless skies and boundless seas,
The embrace of eternity, perfect peace.

The Serene Altar of Connection

In silence, hearts converge and bend,
A whispered prayer, to God we send.
In unity, our spirits rise,
A tranquil grace beneath the skies.

Each soul a note in sacred song,
Together where we all belong.
With gentle hands, we lift our plea,
A bond divine, we long to see.

Forgiveness flows like rivers wide,
In every tear, our love abides.
At this altar, fears dissolve,
In faith's embrace, we find resolve.

The light of love forever shines,
In every act, the truth aligns.
As branches reach, so too, we grow,
In sacred soil, our roots bestow.

Through storms of doubt, we stand as one,
In myriad shadows, we find the sun.
Together here, our spirits soar,
In connection's glow, we seek for more.

Sacred Threads of Unity

In woven fabric, life entwined,
Each thread a gift, in love designed.
With colors bright, we stitch our fate,
A tapestry we celebrate.

Through trials faced, we stand as one,
In every heartbeat, we're begun.
No distance too great to divide,
In sacred threads, we will abide.

As we gather 'round the flame,
No two are lost, yet all the same.
Anointed souls in shared embrace,
With every touch, we find our place.

The silver linings, we behold,
In stories shared and truths untold.
Though storms may rage, our hearts stay true,
In sacred bonds, we will renew.

With every prayer, we intertwine,
Across the ages, love's design.
In unity, our spirits thrive,
Together in this truth, alive.

Visions of Harmonious Faith

In gentle whispers, echoes call,
Together in the rise and fall.
Through every doubt, a star will gleam,
In faith, we find the strength to dream.

With open hearts, we seek the light,
Guided by love in the darkest night.
Each vision shared births hope anew,
In harmony, our souls are true.

A sacred dance, the world we weave,
In every breath, we choose to believe.
Through trials faced, we stand as one,
In faith's embrace, our fears are done.

As birds in flight, we break the chains,
In unity, our love remains.
With lifted hands, we pave the way,
Towards brighter dawns, a brand new day.

In visions clear, our purpose finds,
The path of peace that love unwinds.
Together here, we'll find our grace,
In harmonies, our spirits trace.

The Resurrection of Affection

From ashes rise each heart anew,
In love's embrace, we find our view.
With every tear, a seed is sown,
In fertile ground, affection grown.

The past, it fades, yet still it calls,
In memory's light, our spirit sprawls.
Through every challenge, we reclaim,
A bond reborn, an endless flame.

With tender words and gentle touch,
We heal the wounds that hurt so much.
In circles close, we turn and sway,
In resurrection, love will stay.

In every heartbeat, rhythms blend,
A journey shared that will not end.
As rivers flow to oceans wide,
In love's embrace, we will abide.

And in this sacred space we meet,
Life's greatest gift, so pure and sweet.
Together here, we rise once more,
Our affection blooms, forevermore.

The Sacred Bond

In quiet prayers we find our way,
A tethered heart on holy ground.
With every breath, our spirits sway,
In love's embrace, we're truly bound.

From distant realms, a voice will call,
To guide us through the darkest night.
With faith as wings, we rise, we fall,
Yet in His grace, we find our light.

In trials faced, we learn to trust,
The sacred bond that will not break.
In hope we stand, in love we must,
For every vow, His path we'll take.

United souls in gentle grace,
We walk in step as one divine.
With faith anew, we seek His face,
Together, intertwined, we shine.

So let us sing, both loud and clear,
Of love that binds us, strong and true.
In every heartbeat, He is near,
The sacred bond, forever new.

Seraphic Love's Touch

In twilight's glow, the angels sing,
Of love that dwells in every heart.
A gentle hand on fragile wing,
From earthly ties, we shall not part.

Each whispered prayer, a thread that weaves,
A tapestry of hopes and dreams.
Through trials faced, one never leaves,
In seraphic love, our spirit gleams.

With every tear, a lesson learned,
In fervent grace, our souls embrace.
The sacred fires within us burned,
Ignite the darkness with His grace.

We seek the light in shadows cast,
A promise kept, our faith renewed.
In seraphic love, we hold steadfast,
The sacred bond in hearts imbued.

So let love reign, and hearts unfold,
In every moment, truth we find.
With seraphic love, our lives behold,
A touch divine in hearts aligned.

Whispers of Divine Grace

In quiet moments, softly spoken,
The whispers of divine embrace.
With every word, a chain unbroken,
In stillness found, we seek His face.

Through trials faced and fears unfurled,
His gentle hand will guide us through.
In every heart, a sacred world,
Where grace abounds and love is true.

With every dawn, new mercies rise,
A testament to hope's sweet song.
A light will shine, in darkened skies,
In whispers soft, we all belong.

Through valleys deep, His love endures,
A balm for wounds, a healing grace.
In every soul, His peace assures,
A whisper soothed, a warm embrace.

Let hearts unite in joyful cheer,
For grace has come to set us free.
In whispers borne, we'll persevere,
With love divine, eternally.

A Light Through the Shadows

When darkness falls, a light shall gleam,
A beacon bright, our guiding star.
Through trials faced, through every dream,
His love will lead us, near or far.

In shadows cast, we look for hope,
Upon His words, our faith does stand.
Through every storm, we learn to cope,
With open hearts, we clasp His hand.

The path may wind and twist away,
Yet in His grace, we find our way.
With each small step, we dare to say,
A light through shadows, come what may.

In unity, we gather near,
Embracing love, our spirits soar.
We chase the whispers, overcome fear,
For in His light, we are made whole.

So let the shadows play their game,
For faith ignites the flame anew.
A light shall shine, our hearts aflame,
In every soul, His love shines through.

The Gentle Hand of Providence

In quiet dawn the soft light fades,
A whisper blooms where faith cascades.
The gentle hand that guides our way,
In shadows deep, we find our stay.

With every step, a purpose known,
Each path we tread, the seeds are sown.
In trials faced, our hearts align,
For in His grace, our spirits shine.

Illuminated Souls

In stillness bright, the truth awakes,
With every prayer, the spirit shakes.
A light shines forth, divinely cast,
Illuminating hearts steadfast.

Through storms we walk, our faith the guide,
In unity, we shall abide.
With love as armor, bold and true,
Illuminated, we rise anew.

Harmony Forged in Hope

In every heart, a song remains,
A harmony that breaks the chains.
Through trials faced, we learn to sing,
As hope's sweet voice our spirits bring.

With voices raised in pure embrace,
We celebrate divine grace.
Together strong, we'll find the way,
In harmony, we rise each day.

Redemption's Tender Song

In darkest nights, a melody,
With every note, we are set free.
Redemption sings in soft refrain,
Through every loss, through every pain.

A tender voice calls from above,
Reminding us of boundless love.
In every heart, the truth resounds,
In redemption's arms, our hope is found.

Celestial Healing

In the silence of the night, we pray,
For wounds of the heart to fade away.
Starlight whispers softly, divine,
Embracing souls, the love they find.

Gentle hands from heaven's reach,
In tender moments, they teach.
A balm of hope, forever true,
Brings peace to the lost, renews the view.

With every breath, the spirit's call,
In unity, we rise, we fall.
In healing light, our burdens shed,
In sacred circles, love we spread.

O Nature's grace, your wisdom flows,
In gardens where the mercy grows.
Celestial visions guide our way,
Towards the dawn of a new day.

Sacred Fires of Passion

From ancient wood and kindling bright,
We kindle flames that burn alight.
In the hearth of desire's embrace,
We find our truth, we claim our space.

Passions rise like phoenix flight,
In fervor deep, we seek the light.
The sacred fires, they dance and play,
In hearts awakened, come what may.

Through trials faced and dreams pursued,
In every moment, love imbued.
The sparks ignite our fervent song,
In sacred union, we belong.

With gratitude, we raise our hands,
For every blessing that life grants.
Within this flame, our spirits soar,
In love's embrace, forevermore.

An Offering of Grace

In humble hearts, we gather near,
To share the love, the hope, the cheer.
An offering made with open hands,
In faith we stand, as He commands.

With every word, let kindness flow,
In gentle whispers, truth we sow.
A tapestry of souls entwined,
In unity, our hearts aligned.

Grace illuminates our darkest night,
A compass guiding to the light.
In each embrace, a sacred trust,
In love, in faith, we rise, we must.

Together we transform the pain,
Through every loss, through every gain.
An offering pure, a tapestry,
In grace united, we are free.

The Oasis of Forgiveness

In the desert of our weary hearts,
Forgiveness flows and healing starts.
The oasis blooms with soothing grace,
A refuge found in love's embrace.

With open arms, we seek to mend,
Transforming wounds that time can't bend.
In mercy's light, we lay our fears,
And wash away the silent tears.

Together in this sacred space,
We learn the art of softening grace.
With every step, release the past,
In the moment, true peace amassed.

The waters run clear, our hearts made whole,
A gentle balm for the weary soul.
In the oasis, we find our way,
With loving kindness, come what may.

Rebirth Through Devotion

In the silence of the night, we pray,
Awake the soul, lead the way.
Casting shadows from the past,
In devotion, our hearts are steadfast.

With every tear that graces the ground,
New life blooms where love is found.
Faith ignites the spirit's spark,
Guiding us through the darkest dark.

Renewed in spirit, we rise anew,
In the light of grace, we break through.
The chains of doubt begin to fall,
Through devotion, we answer the call.

In surrender, we find our peace,
From life's struggles, we seek release.
With open hearts, we turn the page,
Reborn in love, we are all sage.

Together we journey, hand in hand,
In faith's embrace, we make our stand.
Through each season, our spirits soar,
In rebirth, we are forevermore.

Threads of Compassion

In the fabric of life, we weave,
Threads of compassion, we believe.
Each stitch a kindness, softly made,
In the hearts of others, love's cascade.

With gentle hands, we mend the tears,
In every sorrow, our spirit cares.
A tapestry of hope unfurls,
Bringing light to distant worlds.

Through trials faced, we stand as one,
With every battle, a victory won.
Hand in hand, we tend the fray,
In threads of compassion, we find our way.

As woven hearts embrace the pain,
New growth arises from the rain.
In unity, we share the load,
Through love's tapestry, we are bestowed.

With every act, we shape the dawn,
In compassion's light, we carry on.
Together, we rise, forever blessed,
In the threads of love, we find our rest.

Wings of Mercy

In the stillness of the heart, we find,
Wings of mercy, ever kind.
Soaring high above the strife,
Carrying hopes, breathing life.

Through the storms, our spirits lift,
In every challenge, a gentle gift.
With open arms, we heal the weak,
In wings of mercy, love we seek.

Like eagles bold, we rise and soar,
In each spirit, we open the door.
Bearing burdens, lightening the load,
On wings of mercy, we travel the road.

With whispers soft, we lend our care,
In every sorrow, we choose to share.
Together, we journey through the night,
In mercy's grace, we find our light.

In acts of kindness, our spirits embrace,
Wings of mercy bring forth grace.
Bound as one, we find our way,
Through love's strong wings, we'll never stray.

The Sanctity of Togetherness

In the circle of life, we gather near,
Embraced in love, we hold so dear.
With every heart, a sacred space,
In togetherness, we find our grace.

Through laughter shared and tears we shed,
In moments precious, souls are fed.
A bond unbroken, we learn to see,
In togetherness, we are set free.

Hand in hand, we face the strife,
In shared journeys, we honor life.
With every story, we weave the thread,
In togetherness, we forge ahead.

As seasons change and time moves on,
Together, we find we're never alone.
In unity's strength, we rise and stand,
In the sanctity of togetherness, hand in hand.

With love's embrace, our spirits sing,
In togetherness, we discover the spring.
A sacred dance, we all partake,
In the heart of togetherness, we awake.

Harbor of Hope

In the stillness of the night,
Anchored hearts seek the light.
Faith a beacon, ever bright,
Guiding souls with pure insight.

Waves of sorrow, cast away,
On the dawn of new-found day.
Strength in prayer, night and day,
God's embrace will always stay.

Whispers of the sacred sea,
Promising eternity.
In this harbor, we are free,
Cradled by divinity.

Tides of worry, ebb and flow,
Yet love's compass points the way.
In each storm, our spirits grow,
Trust the path that God will show.

Look for hope in every heart,
From the dark, we shall not part.
In this journey, we'll embark,
Finding light within the dark.

Ethereal Whirlwind

In the whirlwind of the soul,
Dancing winds make us whole.
Lift our spirits, raise us high,
In the dance where angels fly.

Veils of mist, a gentle shroud,
Comfort whispered soft and loud.
Every breath a prayer we send,
In this storm, we find a friend.

Colors swirl, divine design,
In this chaos, hearts align.
Seek the truth in every gust,
In His mercy, place our trust.

Every moment, holy grace,
Presence felt in time and space.
Ethereal, Your love expands,
Guiding us with sacred hands.

When we falter, when we fail,
On the winds, Your love prevails.
Eternal spirit, guide our way,
In the whirlwind, make us sway.

Echoes in Eternity

In the silence, whispers call,
Echoes soft, a sacred thrall.
Time does fade, yet love remains,
In our hearts, eternal chains.

Every prayer, a voice aloud,
Rising up above the crowd.
Through the ages, faith will stand,
Binding all with gentle hand.

Memories of the divine,
Flow like rivers, intertwine.
Past and future, here they meet,
In each heartbeat, love's retreat.

Life is but a fleeting breath,
Yet in spirit, never death.
Through the shadow, light will glide,
In His presence, we abide.

Echoes linger, soft and clear,
Filling hearts with summer cheer.
In the quiet, hear the song,
In eternity, we belong.

The Sacred River of Us

Flowing gently, time does weave,
In this river, we believe.
Every pebble, tale untold,
In its currents, love unfolds.

Winds of change, both fierce and kind,
In these waters, peace we find.
Let the sacred streams unite,
In this journey, hearts take flight.

Whirling eddies, spirits soar,
Turning tides, we seek the shore.
Every wave, a promise made,
In His love, we are remade.

Cascade of blessings, pure and bright,
Nurturing our souls each night.
In the depths, our secrets swim,
In His light, our hopes begin.

O sacred river, flow so true,
With each sigh, we turn to You.
In this grace, forever trust,
We are one, the sacred us.

Radiant Mending

In the hush of twilight's grace,
Voices whisper, hearts embrace.
Threads of gold weave through the night,
Bringing shattered hopes to light.

Hands uplifted, prayers take flight,
Beneath the stars, we seek the right.
Wounds that bleed shall softly heal,
In unity, our truths reveal.

Grace descends like morning dew,
Each soul cherished, each heart true.
With every tear, a bond shall form,
Together weather any storm.

In sacred circles, we convene,
To find the love that's always been.
Through trials faced and laughter shared,
In this mending, we are bared.

As shadows wane, we stand as whole,
A testament of faith and soul.
In radiant light, we find our way,
To brighter dawns and endless day.

The Sacred Exchange

In the stillness, voices soar,
Hearts in rhythm, evermore.
Each glance a prayer, each word, a vow,
In presence felt, we honor now.

Beneath the weight of life's design,
We trade our burdens, yours and mine.
In kindness offered, gifts unfold,
Love's gentle power, pure and bold.

With every smile, a spark ignites,
Transforming darkness into lights.
We weave connection, strand by strand,
A sacred exchange, hand in hand.

Beneath the veil, we see the truth,
Love's pure essence, forever youth.
From shared embraces, wisdom flows,
In giving freely, our spirit grows.

In the dance of souls, we traverse,
Eternal cycles, love's universe.
Through sacrifice, our hearts rearrange,
In the beauty found, we find the change.

Love's Gentle Restoration

In silence deep, where spirits meet,
Love's gentle touch makes us complete.
Healing waters, pure and clear,
Wash away our doubt and fear.

Through every trial that we face,
Divine compassion finds its place.
In simple graces, life is shared,
Together we rise, forever prepared.

With softest whispers in the night,
Hearts align in sacred light.
From ashes rise, renewed and whole,
Love's gentle restoration of the soul.

In laughter's echo, joy is spun,
We find our strength when we are one.
With hands embraced, we stand as free,
A tapestry of mystery.

As seasons change, our spirits grow,
In kindness shared, our love will flow.
A testament to hearts that roam,
In love's embrace, we find our home.

A Union of Miracles

In every sunrise, hope reborn,
With each new day, our spirits worn.
Miracles dwell in every heart,
In faith and love, we play our part.

Through valleys low and mountains high,
We journey forth, our spirits fly.
A union formed from trials faced,
In shared joys and grief embraced.

In quiet moments, truths arise,
Shining bright beneath the skies.
With open hearts and hands that share,
We find the light in answered prayer.

From scattered seeds, our dreams take flight,
Boundless colors in the night.
With every laugh, a miracle found,
In love's soft whispers, we are crowned.

Together woven, a masterpiece,
In unity, we find our peace.
A testament of grace we'll write,
In this divine, eternal light.

Garden of Restoration

In the garden where shadows fade,
Hope arises, in sunlight laid.
Each flower whispers a sacred song,
In the embrace of where we belong.

Roots intertwine with divine grace,
Healing touch in every place.
From ashes, beauty starts to bloom,
A testament to life's sweet loom.

We sow seeds with faith in hand,
Nurtured by love, in this land.
Tears become raindrops of light,
Transforming the dark into bright.

In this garden, we find our way,
Guided by faith, come what may.
Each step onward, a prayer's release,
In the garden, we find our peace.

Serene Waters of Grace

By the waters, calm and still,
Hearts are healed by His will.
Rippling gently, the truth flows,
In whispers soft, His love glows.

Beneath the sky, so vast and clear,
Every shadow disappears.
The embrace of grace, a sweet embrace,
Carrying us to a holy place.

With every drop, the soul awakens,
To the path of joy unshaken.
Faith, a vessel sailing free,
In serene waters, we come to be.

In reflection, we find our worth,
Each moment cherished, a new birth.
As waters flow, our spirits rise,
Lifted high to the endless skies.

Music of the Heart

In silence, the heart begins to sing,
A melody of love, eternal spring.
Notes dance softly in the air,
Filling spaces with ceaseless prayer.

Each chord strummed from the depths within,
Echoes of grace, where love begins.
Harmony flows in gentle streams,
Awakening hope and tender dreams.

In the rhythm of life we sway,
With faith as our guide, we find our way.
Every heartbeat a sacred sound,
In the music of the heart, we are found.

Together we rise, voices in tune,
Beneath the stars and the bright moon.
A symphony of souls entwined,
In love's embrace, we are aligned.

The Prayerful Heart

In the stillness of the dawning light,
A prayerful heart takes flight.
With hands uplifted, eyes upraised,
Whispers of faith, forever praised.

Kneeling low in sacred space,
Finding solace in His grace.
Every word, a gentle plea,
In the depths, we are set free.

Through trials faced and burdens borne,
A prayerful heart, by love is worn.
In every moment, gentle sighs,
He listens close, with patient eyes.

As dawn awakens the world anew,
In prayer, our spirits break through.
With every breath, we seek the light,
The prayerful heart, a beacon bright.

Spirit's Tender Caress

In whispers soft, the spirit calls,
A balm of peace when darkness falls.
With gentle hands, He guides our way,
Through storms of doubt, He'll never sway.

In silence deep, His light does glow,
A sacred warmth, forever flows.
To weary hearts, He brings repose,
In every breath, His love bestows.

Through trials faced, we find our grace,
In every loss, we see His face.
A guardian strong, He holds us near,
In every moment, He is here.

For in His arms, we are made whole,
Restoring faith within the soul.
With every step, His love we trace,
In every glance, the spirit's grace.

So lift your hands, embrace the bliss,
In tender caress, we find our kiss.
For in our hearts, the truth does sing,
The spirit's love, our everything.

The Healing Spirit of Togetherness

In circles drawn, where hearts unite,
A healing song ignites the night.
Together strong, we bear the load,
In shared embrace, we walk the road.

With open hearts, our spirits soar,
In every voice, a calming roar.
In hands held tight, the darkness fades,
The light of love, our fears invades.

When sorrow creeps, and shadows loom,
Together we can clear the gloom.
In laughter shared, the joy regains,
In joyful tears, our strength remains.

For in this bond, our spirits mend,
A sacred trust, we comprehend.
With every step, we find our way,
In unity, we greet the day.

So let us stand, both strong and true,
With love as guide in all we do.
The healing spirit whispers clear,
Together we shall have no fear.

The Journey Home

Through winding paths and trials faced,
In every step, our faith embraced.
A quest for truth, the heart's desire,
The journey home ignites the fire.

With stars as guide, our souls take flight,
In every shadow, there's a light.
With courage strong, we walk the line,
In every moment, love will shine.

For home is not a distant place,
But found within a warm embrace.
With every breath, we draw Him near,
The journey's end, our purpose clear.

In every tear, the joy will rise,
With every heart, we touch the skies.
For in this quest, we find our role,
The journey home, the spirit's goal.

So hold the faith, let love expand,
With open hearts, we make our stand.
In every step, we sing the praise,
The journey home, our lives ablaze.

Threads of the Divine

In tapestry of life, we weave,
With every thread, we dare believe.
The hands of fate, they intertwine,
In every heart, a spark divine.

With colors bright, our stories blend,
In moments shared, we find a friend.
Through trials faced, we learn to soar,
In love's embrace, we are much more.

For every thread holds ancient grace,
A sacred touch in time and space.
With gentle strength, we hold the line,
Together woven, souls align.

In every stitch, a tale we tell,
Of joy and pain, of rise and fell.
Through laughter, tears, and dreams we find,
The endless dance of the divine.

So let us stand, as one we shine,
In every heart, the love entwines.
For in this weave, our spirits bind,
Threads of the divine, forever kind.

The Alchemy of Affection

In the heart's still chamber, love resides,
Transforming pain to gentle grace.
With every whispered prayer, it guides,
Through shadows, seeking light's embrace.

Hands lifted high, in trust we stand,
A sacred bond, so pure, divine.
With every touch, a healing hand,
Love's alchemy, where we align.

In kindred spirits, we find peace,
A mystic dance of soul to soul.
As doubts dissolve, our sorrows cease,
In love's embrace, we are made whole.

Affection blooms like morning dew,
Awakening the heart anew.
In unity, we find our way,
Together, blessed in every day.

And when the world feels cold and bare,
We hold each other, strong and true.
In every moment, in each prayer,
The alchemy of love shines through.

Unseen Blessings

In quiet corners, grace unfolds,
A gentle hand in unseen ways.
With each small moment, love, it holds,
Transforming hearts through trials and days.

Beneath the surface, faith will rise,
A whispered promise in the night.
Though veils obscure our seeking eyes,
Blessings shimmer, soft and bright.

In every tear, a drop of light,
In every struggle, strength is found.
Through pain and joy, our spirits fight,
For unseen blessings come around.

As petals open to the sun,
Revealing beauty in their claim,
We find that life is gently spun,
With faith our hearts will bear the flame.

So let us wander, hand in hand,
Embracing grace, though hard it seems.
For in this journey, we will stand,
In love, we weave delightful dreams.

Resurrecting Hope

From ashes rise, the spirit bold,
In shadows cast by doubt and fear.
Through trials faced, new stories told,
Resurrection whispers ever near.

In barren fields, a seed takes hold,
Nurtured by faith, through storms we tread.
With every trial, our hearts behold,
The strength within, where hope is fed.

Each dawn unfolds with promise bright,
Reclaiming dreams that seemed out of touch.
In every heart, ignites a light,
A gentle flame that means so much.

With open arms, we face the storm,
Embracing change, the path appears.
With every step, we feel the warm,
Resurrected hope wipes all our tears.

So let us soar on wings of grace,
As love and faith our spirits lift.
Together, finding our sacred place,
Resurrecting hope, our greatest gift.

The Light Beyond Darkness

In shadows deep, a flicker glows,
A promise held through trials faced.
The heart, it knows the way that flows,
To find the light in darkness, grace.

With whispered prayers, the soul ascends,
Through valleys low, we seek the height.
In unity, our strength transcends,
Together, we embrace the light.

As storms may rage and fears arise,
In faith, we stand, we shall not break.
The truth of love shall pierce the skies,
With every dawn, our spirits wake.

And though the night may linger long,
We hold the flame of hope so dear.
For in each heart, a sacred song,
The light beyond shall draw us near.

So let us walk this sacred path,
With courage bright and hearts so strong.
In love's embrace, we'll find the math,
The light beyond will guide us along.

Threads of Unity

In the fabric of life we weave,
Each thread a story we believe.
Hand in hand, hearts align,
Together, forever, we intertwine.

Through trials faced and joys we share,
In unity, we rise, we care.
A tapestry rich, diverse and wide,
Guided by faith, let love be our guide.

From mountains high to valleys low,
In every heart, the spirit will flow.
We gather as one, strong and free,
In this bond, our strength will be.

In laughter and tears, in peace and strife,
We honor the pulse of sacred life.
By grace we stand, by grace we see,
A world united in harmony.

So let us walk with hearts aflame,
In the name of love, we call His name.
With every step, we draw more near,
Threads of unity banish fear.

The Divine Touch

In silence, a whisper, a gentle grace,
The Divine touch we long to embrace.
A light in shadows, a spark anew,
In every moment, He walks with you.

With open hearts, we seek and find,
The sacred truth, the love divine.
In every breath, His presence near,
A soft assurance, calming our fear.

When burdens weight and hope feels lost,
The Divine touch heals at any cost.
Through trials faced, we rise and soar,
Faith like a river, forever more.

In kindness shared, His love displayed,
In every act, His heart conveyed.
A hand extended, a soul set free,
In the Divine touch, we find our plea.

So let your spirit rise and sing,
Embrace the warmth that love can bring.
With each connection, a world reborn,
In the Divine touch, new life is sworn.

The Way Back to Us

In the stillness of night, we seek the thread,
The way back to us, where love is spread.
Through whispers of kindness, we find our way,
A path illuminated, come what may.

In wandering hearts, we search for grace,
In every encounter, we find our place.
With understanding, we heal the scars,
Bringing us closer to the shining stars.

In shadows that linger, hope ignites,
The way back to us, through darkened nights.
With hands held tight, we journey forth,
Rediscovering joy, in love's great worth.

In laughter shared and tears that flow,
The way back to us in the love we show.
Through trials and storms, we find the light,
Guided by faith, dispelling the night.

So let us walk with courage, bold,
In our hearts, a story told.
The way back to us, forever true,
In every moment, I choose you.

Tides of Grace

Like the ocean's waves that dance and flow,
Tides of grace in sun's warm glow.
They rise and fall, a rhythm sweet,
In every heartbeat, love's retreat.

In moments fleeting, we pause to see,
The tides of grace that set us free.
With every breath, we take our stand,
A journey guided by a higher hand.

Through trials faced, in storms we trust,
In tides of grace, our spirits adjust.
With faith as anchor, we hold on tight,
Navigating darkness, seeking the light.

So let us rise with the morning sun,
Embracing the dawn, our spirits run.
In unity, we dance with grace,
As love surrounds us in this sacred space.

The tides of grace, they ebb and flow,
In their embrace, we come to know.
With every wave, a promise made,
In the tides of grace, we are remade.

In the Name of Love's Comfort

In silence vast, we find a light,
A beacon shining through the night.
In tender grace, we feel the sway,
Of love's embrace, come what may.

In trials faced, we stand as one,
With faith ablaze, our hearts begun.
Through whispered prayers, our spirits soar,
In love we find what we implore.

With every tear, divinely shed,
A tapestry where souls were led.
The warmth of grace, a gentle hue,
In love's sweet name, we journey through.

Upon the winds, our voices blend,
In harmony, our hearts extend.
In love's warm arms, we find our peace,
A sacred bond that shall not cease.

Together we shall rise above,
In unity, we speak of love.
With open hearts and hands we strive,
In love's comfort, we are alive.

The Pathway to Salvation

Upon the road that leads us home,
In faith we walk, no more to roam.
Through trials deep and shadows wide,
In love's embrace, we shall abide.

Each step we take, a prayer we speak,
In humble hearts, we find the meek.
With every choice, we seek the light,
In love's pure gift, we find our sight.

Above the clouds, the heavens gleam,
In faith we trust, we dare to dream.
Through stormy nights and endless days,
In love, we find our guiding ways.

The path is long, yet never lone,
In sacred bonds, true hearts have grown.
With every soul, in unity,
Together we claim our destiny.

At journey's end, the gates will part,
With love, they hold the purest heart.
Salvation found, as spirits rise,
In grace, we bask beneath the skies.

Celestial Concord

In heaven's choir, sweet voices meet,
In harmony, the heart's retreat.
With every note, the angels play,
A symphony that guides our way.

In fields of light, where spirits roam,
We find our peace, our true home.
With every breath, a song to share,
In love's embrace, a world laid bare.

The stars above, they twinkle bright,
In cosmic dance, they bring delight.
Together woven, night and day,
In love's vast arms, we softly sway.

With open hearts, we join the throng,
In unity, we sing the song.
Each soul entwined, a sacred thread,
In celestial light, we shall be led.

Through realms of grace, we'll travel far,
In love's embrace, our guiding star.
With every heartbeat, we're renewed,
In concord's glow, our spirits brewed.

Love as Divine Remedy

In every wound, love's balm will heal,
A tender touch that fate will seal.
Through trials faced, with faith we rise,
In love's embrace, the heart complies.

The shadows fade, the light appears,
In love's soft whisper, calm our fears.
With every gesture, kindness flows,
A sacred bond that gently grows.

With open arms, we hold the lost,
In loving grace, we pay the cost.
A guiding hand, a gentle word,
In love's sweet essence, hope is stirred.

Each soul unique, yet intertwined,
In love's pure light, true peace we find.
With every heartbeat, love will mend,
In timeless ways, our hearts transcend.

Together we shall share this fate,
In love's embrace, we cultivate.
As remedy divine, it shines above,
In every moment, we choose love.

Faithful Hearts Unite

In sacred bonds, our spirits blend,
With faith as light, we shall transcend.
Together strong, we face the day,
In harmony, we choose to pray.

With joy we gather, hands entwined,
In love's embrace, our hearts aligned.
Each whispered prayer, a gentle breath,
In unity, we find our strength.

The promise shines like morning dew,
With every step, we walk renew.
Guided by grace, we rise above,
In faithful hearts, we share our love.

Through trials fierce and shadows cast,
Our vision clear, our spirits steadfast.
In worship's glow, we seek the truth,
Together we stand, forever couth.

Let faith resound, a joyful song,
In every heart, where we belong.
Together now, let voices soar,
In faithful hearts, forevermore.

Reverent Yearning

In quiet moments, souls aspire,
To seek the light, a heart's desire.
With open hands, we seek the grace,
In humble prayers, we find our place.

The longing deep, a sacred call,
To rise above, to never fall.
Through trials faced, we stand secure,
In faith and love, our hearts endure.

A whisper soft, the spirit's plea,
For peace to reign eternally.
In reverent tones, we softly sing,
In every heart, hope takes wing.

Beneath the stars, we dream and yearn,
With every breath, our souls discern.
An endless quest for truth and light,
In reverent yearning, hearts take flight.

Together we seek a brighter dawn,
In every challenge, we are drawn.
To share the love that knows no end,
In reverent yearning, we transcend.

A Chalice of Compassion

In the chalice held by grace,
We find our strength, we find our place.
Filled with love, it overflows,
A gift divine, the heart bestows.

With every act of kindness shared,
A flame ignites, our hearts repaired.
In compassion's light, we shall see,
The beauty in humanity.

Together we lift the weary soul,
Embracing all, we make them whole.
For in the depths of every heart,
Compassion lives, it is our art.

Through trials faced, and burdens borne,
In every tear, a hope reborn.
From chalice spills the love we crave,
In every gesture, we can save.

So let us pour this blessed wine,
In every heart, love's grand design.
A chalice raised, let spirits soar,
In compassion's realm, forevermore.

The Path of the Graced

On the path where grace does flow,
We journey forth, no fear to show.
With every step, a blessing found,
In every moment, love profound.

Through winding ways, our spirits glide,
In faith we walk, with God our guide.
With trust in heart, we pave the way,
For in His love, we find our stay.

The road may twist, the shadows may loom,
Yet in our hearts, we banish gloom.
With grace as light, we press ahead,
In every trial, His words are spread.

In unity, we seek the truth,
In joyful hearts, we share our youth.
For on this path, our souls embrace,
The journey blessed, the love of grace.

Through every challenge, we are blessed,
In the heart's embrace, we find our rest.
Hand in hand, we walk as one,
On paths of grace, our work begun.

Wings of Devotion

On sacred winds our spirits soar,
In prayerful whispers we implore.
With hearts uplifted, we find grace,
In love's embrace, we seek His face.

Through trials faced, our faith ignites,
With every turn, divine delights.
In quiet moments, peace we hold,
As angel wings our dreams unfold.

A journey marked by trust divine,
In every heart, His light will shine.
Together bound by sacred ties,
In faith and hope, our spirits rise.

With grateful hearts, our lives we gift,
In serving others, souls we lift.
For love is found in humble deeds,
Each act of kindness, faith proceeds.

So let us fly, on wings of prayer,
In harmony, we thus declare.
For in His love, forever free,
Together in eternity.

The Healing Light of Faith

In shadows deep, despair may dwell,
Yet faith will break the darkest spell.
A gentle hand, a soft embrace,
Light of the world, in every space.

When burdens weigh, and spirits break,
In whispered prayers, our hearts awake.
The healing balm that faith imparts,
Lifts weary souls, mends broken parts.

Through trials faced, we find our way,
In darkest nights, He is our day.
With every tear, a seed is sown,
In gardens rich, our hope has grown.

So let us walk, in love's pure glow,
For in His light, our spirits flow.
Together bound by trust and grace,
In every heart, His light we trace.

In moments sweet, His peace descends,
With every breath, our spirit mends.
For faith, our guide, through every fight,
Will lead us home, to love's pure light.

Divine Tapestry of Us

In threads of life, we intertwine,
A sacred pattern, by design.
With colors bright and shadows deep,
A tapestry of love we keep.

Each story told, a stitch so fine,
In laughter shared, our hearts align.
With every joy, and every plight,
Together weaving, pure delight.

For in this space, we find our role,
A canvas graced, a perfect whole.
Bound by a love that never fades,
In unity, our strength cascades.

Through trials faced, our bonds will grow,
In faith and love, we surely know.
For every thread, both light and dark,
Creates the masterpiece, the spark.

So let us stitch with tender hands,
The stories told of sacred lands.
In every breath, our joy will rise,
A divine tapestry in the skies.

A Covenant of Serenity

In quiet moments, peace descends,
A sacred pact, where love transcends.
With open hearts, we seek the light,
In harmony, we find our flight.

Through trials faced, we stand as one,
In every dawn, a chance begun.
With gentle words, we choose to heal,
In kindness shown, our hearts reveal.

This covenant, a bond so true,
In every storm, we will renew.
For love's embrace, a guiding star,
Together, dear, we'll travel far.

With thankful hearts, beneath the sky,
In moments sweet, our spirits fly.
For in His grace, we find our way,
Through every night, into the day.

So let us walk, in peace and joy,
A covenant that none destroy.
In faith and love, we now decree,
Together, in sweet unity.

Anointed Journeys

In the shadow of grace, I tread softly,
Paths illuminated by the holy light.
With each step, a whisper of mercy,
Guiding my heart through the night.

Blessed are those who seek true wisdom,
With faith as their sturdy guide.
Each trial, a lesson in the kingdom,
Anointed journeys with God by my side.

Mountains rise, yet fear can't hold me,
For I am cradled in divine embrace.
The trials faced only mold me,
As I walk in His enduring grace.

In the stillness, the voice of the Savior,
Calls my spirit to rise and sing.
Trusting fully, filled with favor,
In His love, I find everything.

With each dawn, new hope arises,
To shine on the weary and weak.
Anointed journeys lead to surprises,
Where hearts find strength in the meek.

Blossoms of Compassion

In gardens of faith, we plant seeds,
Nurtured by love and tender care.
Each blossom grows from heartfelt deeds,
A sign of grace, beyond compare.

The fragrance spreads through every soul,
A reminder of kindness, pure and bright.
With open hands, we become whole,
Fostering hope in the darkest night.

When burdens weigh on weary shoulders,
Compassion blooms in gentle hearts.
With courage, our mission only bolders,
As we strive to play our parts.

Through storms, we stand, united strong,
Fearless in love, we shall not fall.
The melody of kindness sings along,
A sweet refrain we hear call.

In every smile, a story found,
Woven in threads of faith and trust.
Blossoms of compassion all around,
Transforming our world, as it must.

Promises of the Soul

Beneath the stars, a promise lingers,
Whispered gently to the night.
The heart, a compass, it always fingers,
Guiding toward the sacred light.

With every prayer, a vow I make,
To seek the truth in every breath.
Through trials faced and bonds we break,
Our souls united, conquering death.

In quiet spaces, where spirits dwell,
Promises are woven through the years.
Each tear a story, a sacred spell,
Cleansing the heart, washing away fears.

Faith is the anchor in raging seas,
Stirring hope where doubt may arise.
In the depth of despair, we find ease,
For love's embrace never denies.

With grace as our witness, we stand tall,
Intent on living the truth we've heard.
Promises of the soul, cherished by all,
In unity, life becomes our word.

Wings of Redemption

With wings of redemption, we take flight,
Soaring on winds of grace and hope.
The burden of sin fades from our sight,
In His love, we learn to cope.

Every stumble, a chance to rise,
In forgiveness, we find our worth.
Through tears and trials, the spirit cries,
A testimony of rebirth.

The chains that bind begin to break,
As faith ignites the flames of change.
With every vow, a promise we make,
Life's beauty becomes less strange.

In moments of darkness, we find the light,
Guided by love's unwavering call.
Wings of redemption share their might,
Lifting souls, never to fall.

With our hearts uncovered, we embrace the way,
Leading others to the path we've cross.
In the dance of hope, we shall not sway,
For redemption's wings conquer every loss.

Eternal Echoes of Affection

In the silence of the night, we pray,
Hearts connected in a sacred way,
Love descends like a gentle breeze,
Whispering comfort, granting ease.

Through trials faced and mountains steep,
In His promise, our spirits leap,
A bond unbroken, through joy and strife,
Eternal echoes, the song of life.

In unity, we gather as one,
Under the gaze of an endless sun,
Through faith we rise, unchained, set free,
In love's embrace, we find our key.

Celestial visions, our souls ignite,
Guided by grace, we seek the light,
With every heartbeat, a prayer we send,
In the arms of hope, we shall transcend.

Together we stand, hearts intertwined,
In the tapestry of love, we find,
The sacred truth, forever near,
Echoes of affection, purer than fear.

Beneath the Stars, We Mend

Beneath the stars, our spirits rise,
In the stillness, we find our ties,
Each twinkle, a promise from above,
Binding our hearts in a dance of love.

In the twilight, shadows take flight,
Guided by faith, we chase the light,
Whispers of grace fill the night air,
In His presence, we lay our cares.

With open arms, He welcomes us home,
In the vast unknown, we are not alone,
Every tear shed, a seed we sow,
In His garden, the love will grow.

As the moon holds the night's embrace,
We mend our souls in His warm grace,
With every heartbeat, we cherish the night,
Beneath the stars, our spirits unite.

Together we journey, hand in hand,
Weaving our dreams through this sacred land,
In every moment, His love we send,
Beneath the stars, together we mend.

Harbors of Healing Justice

In the harbor of light, we find reprieve,
A sanctuary where we dare believe,
With hearts aglow, we seek the path,
In justice's arms, we escape the wrath.

Through storms that rage and trials that test,
In faith's embrace, we find our rest,
With every act of kindness sown,
A world transformed, to us is shown.

Justice flows like a river wide,
Nurturing hope, the wounded beside,
Each voice united, a resounding song,
In healing justice, we all belong.

With compassion as our guiding star,
We journey onward, no matter how far,
Together we rise, with hearts aligned,
In the embrace of justice, our souls refined.

In this harbor, we take a stand,
For every heart, we join our hands,
Creating a future, bright and just,
In the light of love, we place our trust.

Sacred Melodies of Rebirth

In the dawn's glow, new hope is born,
With melodies sweet, the spirit's worn,
Each note a whisper, a gentle call,
In sacred harmony, we rise and fall.

Through the ashes, we find our way,
Embraced by light, no longer gray,
In every heartbeat, a song so true,
Rebirth ignites the power in you.

With every sunrise, the past released,
Our souls awaken, seeking peace,
Together we sing, a chorus divine,
In the tapestry of life, our threads entwine.

Through trials faced and shadows cast,
We find the strength to break the vast,
In love's embrace, we take a breath,
With sacred melodies, we conquer death.

In the dance of life, we weave our fate,
Rebirth and grace, we celebrate,
In every note, a promise to keep,
In sacred melodies, our spirits leap.

Chosen by the Spirit

In the silence, whispers rise,
Guided paths through stormy skies.
Hearts aflame, a holy light,
Chosen ones walk in the night.

Hands uplifted, prayers ascend,
Faithful souls, on Him depend.
Echoes shimmer in the air,
In His grace, we find our care.

Mountains tremble, valleys sing,
In the depths, His love we bring.
Every burden, cast away,
Chosen paths lead us to stay.

Through trials, spirits rise anew,
Strength bestowed, the hands that do.
In our weakness, power shown,
In His mercy, we are known.

United in a sacred bond,
Every heart to Him is fond.
In the journey, side by side,
In the Spirit, we abide.

Echoes of Forgiveness

In the shadows, voices call,
Whispers of grace, lifting all.
Hearts entangled, wounds set free,
Echoes of love, a sacred plea.

With open arms, we embrace the past,
In forgiveness, freedom's cast.
Chains of sorrow, broken now,
In His light, we humbly bow.

Crosses carried, burdens shared,
Hearts awakened, souls laid bare.
Mercy flows like rivers wide,
In our hearts, grace will abide.

From the ashes, beauty grows,
In forgiveness, love bestows.
Hands held tight, we heal the pain,
United, we'll rise once again.

Lessons learned, we find our way,
With each dawn, a brighter day.
In His name, we find our stance,
Echoing love, a holy dance.

The Soul's Sanctuary

In the stillness, spirits rest,
Seeking solace, we are blessed.
In His presence, peace unfolds,
Love eternal, warmth that holds.

Gentle whispers, hearts awake,
In retreat, our burdens shake.
Silent moments, deep and true,
In the gaze of love, renew.

Amidst the chaos, shelter found,
In His arms, we stand our ground.
Hope ignites like stars at night,
Guiding souls to His pure light.

Through the storms, we seek His face,
In quietude, we find our place.
Every tear, a story told,
In His refuge, hearts turn bold.

As we gather, spirits thrive,
In community, love's alive.
Soul's sanctuary, safe and sound,
In His grace, we are unbound.

Miracles in the Midst of Pain

In the depths, where shadows creep,
Faith awakens, through the weep.
Every heartbeat, a silent prayer,
Miracles dance in the despair.

Through the trials, hope ignites,
In the darkness, guiding lights.
Healing flows, like rivers wide,
In our brokenness, He abides.

Every tear, a seed of grace,
Sprouting joy in barren space.
In the turmoil, strength is born,
Through the fire, we are adorned.

With each struggle, love appears,
Turning sorrow into cheers.
In the pain, our hearts proclaim,
Miracles dwell, calling His name.

On the horizon, dawn will break,
Every trial, a path to take.
Through the pain, the spirit soars,
In His love, our soul restores.

The Lantern of Togetherness

In the glow of faith, we find our way,
Hearts united, come what may.
Together we stand, hand in hand,
Guided by love, a sacred land.

With every prayer, a bond we weave,
In joy and sorrow, we believe.
The lantern brightens the darkest night,
Illuminating paths, shining light.

When shadows fall, we lift each other,
A bond unbroken, sister and brother.
In the warmth of grace, we softly tread,
The whispers of hope, where angels led.

Through trials faced, we grow in trust,
A faith unshaken, in God we must.
With every heartbeat, love's refrain,
Together we rise, through joy and pain.

So let the lantern guide our way,
In unity's voice, together we stay.
With open hearts, we share our song,
In the dance of life, we all belong.

A Whisper from the Divine

In the silence of night, a whisper calls,
From the heavens above, where love enthralls.
It beckons softly, like a gentle breeze,
Awakening hearts, putting souls at ease.

With every breath, a sacred sound,
The heartbeat of grace, in truth we're bound.
In moments of doubt, we seek and find,
The tender embrace of the Divine mind.

Through trials and storms, we seek the light,
In faith we gather, through darkest night.
Each whisper carries a promise clear,
Of comfort and strength, always near.

When paths are shrouded, and we feel lost,
Remember the love that bridges the cost.
In the hush of the night, let hope arise,
With every whisper, the heart complies.

So listen closely, to the still, small voice,
In the dance of faith, let us rejoice.
For in each moment, the spirit's rhyme,
Is the echo of love that transcends time.

Chosen Journeys of the Heart

Each heart a vessel, on journeys vast,
Guided by grace, we hold steadfast.
Through valleys deep and mountains high,
We seek the truth as we journey nigh.

With every step, a purpose born,
In whispers of love, we are reborn.
The sacred path, a winding road,
In faith we carry our shared load.

Through laughter and tears, we carve our place,
In the tapestry of life, woven in grace.
Together we walk, in shadows, in light,
Counting our blessings, shining so bright.

When doubts arise, and storms assail,
We find our strength in love's holy trail.
For every heart holds a story deep,
In chosen journeys, our souls to keep.

So let us cherish the roads we roam,
In unity's bond, we find our home.
With every heartbeat, we make our vow,
To honor the journey, here and now.

The Temple of Togetherness

In the temple of hearts, we gather near,
With love as our altar, we hold dear.
With every prayer, our spirits rise,
A sanctuary built beneath the skies.

In shared silence, we find our song,
In togetherness, we all belong.
Each hand clasped tight, a pledge we give,
In this holy place, we learn to live.

Through trials faced, we share the load,
In every moment, we walk the road.
With kindness woven in every deed,
The temple flourishes; love is the seed.

In laughter's echo and in tears' embrace,
We find our strength, we find our grace.
Through shadows and light, we build our home,
In the temple of togetherness, we roam.

So let us gather, hearts intertwined,
In the bond of love, forever aligned.
For in this sacred space, we shall see,
The beauty of life, in unity.

Celestial Mending

In the silence of night, grace descends,
Healing shadows where sorrow blends.
A whisper of hope, gentle and near,
Restoring the spirit, quieting fear.

With hands of love, the divine impart,
Stitching the fabric of a wounded heart.
Each thread of light, a promise to hold,
Transforming the broken, restoring the bold.

In stillness, we find our spirits align,
Cradled in warmth, in love we entwine.
Celestial mending, a sacred embrace,
Guiding the lost through time and space.

From ashes we rise, reborn and renewed,
With faith as our armor, and gratitude.
Every tear that has fallen, a testament true,
To the mending of hearts, in all that we do.

So let us unite, in this holy light,
For hope shines the brightest in the darkest night.
With a promise of peace, we carry the flame,
Celestial mending, we rise with His name.

Emissaries of Light

In shadows cast where hope seems lost,
Emissaries gather, no matter the cost.
Carrying torches of warmth and grace,
Illuminating paths, a love to embrace.

Through valleys of doubt, with courage they tread,
Whispering truths that the weary have said.
Each heartbeat a rhythm, a drum of the soul,
Restoring the shattered, making us whole.

From mountains high to oceans wide,
They travel together, as angels beside.
In acts of kindness, in words that inspire,
Emissaries of light, we lift hearts higher.

With every touch, a message unfolds,
Life's tapestry woven with stories untold.
In unity's bond, we find our wings,
Emissaries shining, in harmony sings.

So let us discern, in each fleeting glance,
The light in each soul, the divine in each chance.
With love as our guide, together we'll rise,
Emissaries of light, reflecting the skies.

The Touch of a Blessed Heart

When kindness spills from a gentle touch,
The world around us feels loved so much.
A blessed heart beats with tender grace,
Filling the void with warmth and embrace.

In laughter and tears, a promise we share,
Through trials and storms, our hearts laid bare.
With each fleeting moment, our spirits inspire,
The touch of a heart, igniting the fire.

In silence we speak, in glances we find,
The beauty of presence, two souls intertwined.
A whisper of love, in the softest of ways,
The touch of a heart that forever stays.

Through tangled paths, as we wander and roam,
The blessed heart leads us back to our home.
In every embrace, let the healing begin,
For the touch of a heart is where life starts to win.

So cherish the moments, the love we can give,
For that is the essence of how we shall live.
In the grace of our hearts, let compassion impart,
The touch of a blessed heart, a divine work of art.

Ethereal Comfort

Within the stillness, a whisper so sweet,
Ethereal comfort, a soft heartbeat.
Clouds of worry drift far away,
Beneath boundless skies, we find our way.

In gentle caress of the evening breeze,
Our spirits are lifted, we find our ease.
With every moment wrapped in grace,
Ethereal comfort, a sacred space.

Through trials of life, when burdens grow heavy,
The light shines brightly, steady and ready.
In the arms of the night, we rest and believe,
Ethereal comfort, in love we receive.

With stars as our guide, we wander afar,
The cosmos embraces, no matter how far.
In whispers of peace, the heart learns to trust,
Ethereal comfort, in love we must.

So carry this solace wherever we roam,
For within us, we hold our true home.
In every heartbeat, may we find joy,
Ethereal comfort, life's purest deploy.

Embraced by Grace

In shadows deep, where hearts do sigh,
A whisper comes from heaven's high.
With arms outstretched, He calls our name,
Embraced by grace, forever the same.

In trials faced, we find our strength,
As mercy flows in endless length.
A gentle touch upon our soul,
Restoring faith, making us whole.

We wander 'neath the stars at night,
His love a beacon, pure and bright.
Through valleys dark, we walk with peace,
In every breath, His love's release.

When burdens weigh, we come to pray,
With open hearts, we find our way.
In grace we rise, from dust we bloom,
A symphony that chases gloom.

In every moment, grace abound,
In silence sweet, His voice is found.
We dance in light, forever free,
Embraced by grace, He cares for me.

Sunlight on Stormy Waters

When tempest roars and waves do crash,
Our hearts despair, in darkness ash.
Yet in the storm, we feel His might,
Sunlight breaks through, a guiding light.

With every trial, we learn to trust,
In faith we stand, in hope we must.
For every tear, a promise made,
In grace we rise, though shadows fade.

He calms the seas, the winds obey,
In Christ, our peace, our hope to stay.
As sunlight warms both sea and shore,
Our spirits lifted, we sail once more.

In midst of chaos, hear His call,
For in His love, we shall not fall.
With courage bold, we face the night,
Sunlight on waters, our hearts take flight.

Together we stand, hand in hand,
With faith as strong as shifting sand.
The storm will pass, and hope restore,
In heaven's light, we seek no more.

The Balm of Forgiveness

In hearts where sorrow once held sway,
Forgiveness blooms, a brand new day.
With gentle hands, we mend the strife,
The balm of grace revives our life.

The weight of grudges, we set free,
In love's embrace, we choose to be.
Through wounds we share and scars exposed,
Forgiveness flows, our hearts disclosed.

With every breath, we start anew,
In mercy's light, our spirits grew.
As healing pours from heaven's will,
The balm of love, our hearts shall fill.

In tenderness, we seek to share,
The love that heals, beyond compare.
Together united, we walk as one,
In unity, our battles won.

No longer chained by pain or shame,
We rise in hope, we sing His name.
For in forgiveness, there's peace divine,
The balm of grace, forever shine.

Radiance of Reconciliation

In shadows cast by doubt and fear,
Reconciliation draws us near.
With open hearts, we seek the light,
In unity, we shine so bright.

Through valleys low, we find our way,
In every choice, we choose to stay.
For love unites, no longer torn,
In grace reborn, our hearts adorned.

With every step, we learn to bend,
To heal the wounds, to be a friend.
The bonds of peace, like threads entwined,
In harmony, our souls aligned.

Through trials faced and words exchanged,
We find a truth that's long arranged.
With open arms, we share our song,
In reconciliation, we belong.

For in the light of love's embrace,
We journey forth in sacred space.
In every heart, a beacon glows,
Radiance of peace, forever flows.

Milton Keynes UK
Ingram Content Group UK Ltd.
UKHW020042271124
451585UK00012B/1012

9 789916 897973